Where The Three Worlds Touch
The Lives of Abraham Lincoln, Rumi & Shams, and Rab'ia
Through Dramatic Works

Volume 1: Abraham Lincoln
This Dust was Once the Man
Elisabeth Kehl
Nicolas Walker

A Blue Logic Publication
http://bluelogic.us/
All rights reserved © 2011 by
Elisabeth Kehl
Nicolas Walker
Copyright throughout the world

No part of this book may be reproduced or transmitted in any form or by any means, graphic, electronic, or mechanical, including photocopying, recording, taping, or by an information storage retrieval system, without permission in writing from the publisher.

ISBN: 978-0-9835253-7-0

Separation from Him is like falling into a deep well, remembering Him is like a rope. -- **Rumi**

CONTENTS

Notes to the Reader 7 --- Abraham Lincoln: This Dust was Once the Man

NOTES TO THE READER

To the casual observer there is little in common in the lives of Rumi & Shams, Rabi'a, and Abraham Lincoln. Even in the case of Rumi & Shams and Rabi'a; while all three are recognized as Sufis, the two men lived almost 400 years later than Rabi'a, and both were established and well respected Spiritual Leaders of their day. In contrast, Rabi'a was, at different times in her life, an orphan, a slave and a reputed "Lady of the Night."

However, to the spiritual seeker, the connection between all four personages is unmistakable. Christ said "I am the good shepherd; I know my own and my own know me." Sincere aspirants on the Spiritual Path recognize Masters; it can be no other way, as they are striving after the same reality.

So it is that these four individuals are linked by their unwavering pursuit of Spiritual Truth through Self Knowledge. In fact, all Spiritual Wisdom that comes down to us in the form of Teachings are mere by-products of Self Knowledge. If one has not Self-Knowledge, then it cannot be transmitted or taught to another. Differences in era, culture, or gender amongst Spiritual Masters will only produce discrepancies of style or expression but not of substance. We encourage the readers of this volume to search out the connections — rather than notice any supposed differences — in the subjects of these dramas.

****

All three scripts in this book were created for the stage as performance pieces. With that in mind, we have included in the text the original descriptions of props (most of which were ultimately not incorporated into the minimalist sets), lighting cues, exits and entrances, references to music, dance, sounds, etc.

The material used in the play *Rumi & Shams: In their own words* came from various sources. A significant amount of the lines spoken by the characters of Rumi & Shams were their own words, as the title implies. They were collated from various translations of Rumi's poetry and discourses as well as from letters and biographies of the two friends.

In all three scripts, a liberal amount of "artistic license" was employed whenever it aided the script's movement or development. For instance, on a few occasions the character of Shams speaks words from Rumi's writings, and vice versa. On one or two other occasions, if it rang true, we included in the lines of Rumi or Shams a saying of Ibn Arabi or another Sufi Master.

Some of the Characters (namely Rumi's disciples and other minor characters) are inventions of the authors, as are their dialogs. Rumi had two sons. For dramatic purposes they were merged into one character; called Ala Al Din, after his youngest son.

****

The majority of the script for *Abraham Lincoln: This dust was once the man* was drawn from a collection of letters and notes written by Lincoln's friends, colleagues, relatives and acquaintances, assembled by William Herndon, one of his law partners. These *reminiscences* were taken from published manuscripts in their raw, unedited form, just as they were written by the individuals.

In a few instances, the actual author of the recollections is unclear, so no attribution is given. It is obvious that some passages, like the Gettysburg Address, are the words of Lincoln himself, and in those cases, we have placed the name "Lincoln" as the character.

N.W.

Abraham Lincoln:
This Dust was Once the Man

CAST:

Commentator (Composite Character)
Abraham Lincoln
Mary Todd Lincoln
Sarah Bush Lincoln (Abe's Stepmother)
Ulysses S. Grant
Walt Whitman
William Herndon
  John Parker
Other composite Characters
Poetry Reader
Singer

SONGS:
Battle Hymn of the Republic
Dixie

POEM:
When Lilacs Last in the Dooryard Bloom'd
By Walt Whitman

SINGER

Mine eyes have seen the glory of the coming of the Lord:
He is trampling out the vintage where the grapes of wrath are stored;
He hath loosed the fateful lightning of His terrible swift sword:
His truth is marching on.

Glory, glory, hallelujah!
Glory, glory, hallelujah!
Glory, glory, hallelujah!
His truth is marching on.

I have seen Him in the watch-fires of a hundred circling camps,
They have builded Him an altar in the evening dews and damps;
I can read His righteous sentence by the dim and flaring lamps:
His day is marching on.

Glory, glory, hallelujah!
Glory, glory, hallelujah!
Glory, glory, hallelujah!
His day is marching on.

He has sounded forth the trumpet that shall never call retreat;
He is sifting out the hearts of men before His judgment-seat:
Oh, be swift, my soul, to answer Him! be jubilant, my feet!
Our God is marching on.

Glory, glory, hallelujah!
Glory, glory, hallelujah!
Glory, glory, hallelujah!
Our God is marching on.

In the beauty of the lilies Christ was born across the sea,
With a glory in His bosom that transfigures you and me:
As He died to make men holy, let us die to make men free,
While God is marching on.

Glory, glory, hallelujah!
Glory, glory, hallelujah!
Glory, glory, hallelujah!
While God is marching on.

The SONG ENDS and a DRUM in a somber funeral cadence is heard. DRUM ENDS.

READER

When lilacs last in the dooryard bloom'd
And the great star early droop'd in the western sky in the night,
I mourn'd, and yet shall mourn with ever-returning spring.

Ever-returning spring, trinity sure to me you bring,
Lilac blooming perennial and drooping star in the west,
And thought of him I love.

O powerful western fallen star!
O shades of night — O moody, tearful night!
O great star disappear'd — O the black murk that hides the star
O cruel hands that holds me powerless — O helpless sour of me!

O harsh surrounding cloud that will not free my soul.

In the dooryard fronting an old farm-house near the white-washed palings,
Stands the lilac-bush tall-growing with heart-shaped leaves of rich green,
With many a pointed blossom rising delicate, with the perfume strong I love,
With every leaf a miracle — and from this bush in the dooryard,
With delicate — color'd blossoms and heart-shaped leaves of rich green,
A sprig with its flower I break.

Refrain of FUNERAL DRUM CADENCE is heard. DRUM ENDS.

COMMENTATOR

My friends and I come before you on the anniversary of America's birth to pay tribute to a great American—a great leader of men, Abraham Lincoln, who was our 16th president. The people who accompany me today all knew Mr. Lincoln personally; most of us knew him intimately. Today we will share with you our fondest memories and recollections of our friend and President.

In addition to those memories, we also wish to share with you the written words of friends and acquaintances that could not be here today.
Past generations, leading up to yours, have honored his memory and noted his accomplishments well. There are many thousands of books and publications in existence, with more appearing with each passing year.

It is not our aim to call attention to the already well-documented facts regarding his humble origins, his entrance into politics, his political ideology, and his daily routines. These may serve as a backdrop to our gathering—a mere pretext that we will touch upon but lightly.

We come before you to document his sufferings, his failings, his great compassion, his frailty and vulnerability, his courage and that indomitable Will that singlehandedly rescued this nation from the brink of collapse and chaos. These are the trials that reveal the inner man—the completed man—and this is the subject of our proceedings today.

A READER steps forward.

READER

I knew Mr. Lincoln from his days in New Salem. He was a clerk in my grocery store. That's where he first got the name "Honest Abe." Why, one time a man overpaid him four cents and was gone before he noticed it. Before he went to bed that night, Abe walked several miles to repay the pennies. Another time, he did the same thing to make up the deficiency, after having inadvertently used too small a weight in measuring out a pound of tea. (Shakes his head) We, that is, some locals, who mingled around the store, and I, started to tease him about it, and I guess the name stuck.

On more than one occasion, Abe and I took a flatboat together from the Ohio River down the Mississippi to New Orleans to sell our produce. I remember one trip distinctly. The year would have been in 1831, and Abe was about 22 years old. This trip marked his first face-to-face encounter with slavery.

New Orleans was a teeming metropolis, unlike any city we had seen. As it was, the produce market was within a close proximity of the slave auctions that were held on a daily basis. We were curious, so we went over and watched the proceedings.

We watched those black people in chains being inspected like cattle — prodded and poked — watched families being ripped apart — the father sold to one owner, the mother to another, the child to a third. Abe looked on intently, silently. In another area, a vigorous and comely mulatto girl was being sold. She underwent a thorough examination at the hands of the bidders; they pinched her flesh and made her trot up and down like a horse to show how she moved in order, as the auctioneers said, that "bidders might satisfy themselves" whether the article they were buying was sound or not.

Finally, Abe said, "I've seen enough. Let's get away from this." We walked away in silence, drained from the spectacle. Suddenly Abe stopped, looked off in the distance and said, "If I ever get a chance to hit that thing (meaning slavery) I'll hit it, and hit it hard."

COMMENTATOR

Many have suggested that it was the slavery issue that brought Mr. Lincoln into politics. That's not entirely factual. In truth he was born for politics; it was as natural for him as breathing.

Oddly, he was not what you would call a social man — did not like crowds. But when he saw a wrong or injustice, his natural inclination was to rectify it, to set it right. And he knew politics provided that avenue to him. After his first exposure to politics, mainly on a state level, but including one term as a congressman in Washington, he withdrew to private life, studied Law and opened his own Practice. It is true, however, that his re-entrance into politics some years later was largely aided by the threat of repeal of certain national laws which would then insure the spread and expansion of slavery, even outside the Southern states.

You might say at that "crossroad," his fate was sealed. And once back in the political arena, he would get his chance to "hit" slavery and hit it hard.

READER

Death was a recurring theme in Mr. Lincoln's life; it touched him early and often. When he was nine years old, his mother, Nancy, died of a dreaded scourge known as the Milk Sickness. She had helped nurse the wife of a neighbor. The lady died, and Nancy herself suddenly felt ill. Her head swam and sharp pains shot through her abdomen. She seemed to be on fire, calling for water, water, more water.

Finally, she was unable even to raise her head from the pillow, and she could not talk above a whisper. She beckoned Abraham and his sister to her and tried to speak. She pleaded with them to be good to each other, to live as she had taught them, and to worship God. These were her last words, and she finally died on the seventh day of her illness.
Ten years later, Abraham would lose his only blood sibling, his older sister, Sarah, who died at the age of 20 in childbirth.

But perhaps the most difficult of all deaths to cope with was the death of his fiancée Ann Rutledge. Many have said she was not only his first love, but his only true love.

READER

I can vouch for this fact, as he was boarding with my family at the time of Miss Rutledge's death. She was a woman of exquisite beauty and sharp intellect – deep and philosophic. Brilliant, I would say. She had a gentle and kind heart – full of love and sympathy. Her character was more than good: it was noted throughout the county.

A short time before their marriage was to take place, she came down with Typhoid fever and died in 4 or 5 days. The shock was so sudden, Mr. Lincoln had to be locked up by his friends to prevent derangement or suicide – so hard did he take her death.

One day shortly after her burial, it rained. Mr. Lincoln said he could not bear the idea of its raining on her grave. That was the time the community said he was crazy. He was not crazy, but he was despondent a very long time. I think this was in the year of 34 or 35.

COMMENTATOR

I might add, however, that if Mr. Lincoln had married Ann Rutledge, in all probability he would have been happy, but he would not have been President. He was deliberate in thought and movement, and Ann was not the type that would have driven him to achieve political distinction. But Mary Todd, obsessed with an undying determination to live in the White House, was no sooner married to Lincoln than she had him out running for Congress again. In fact, she once predicted almost 15 years before the fact that he would become President of the United States.

MARY TODD LINCOLN

Yes, he is a great favorite everywhere. He is to be president of the United States some day; if I had not thought so I never would have married him, for you can see he is not pretty. But look at him! Doesn't he look as if he would make a magnificent president?

COMMENTATOR

On the contrary, to me he looked about as unpromising a candidate as I could well imagine the American people were ever likely to put forward. I must confess at that time I did not thoroughly know the man or his capabilities. But death would follow Mr. Lincoln for a long time. He was still to bury two of his four sons; Edward aged 4 and Willie, his favorite, aged 11. Willie, to this day, is the only child of a President to die inside the White house.

By the time the Great War came to an end, Death would visit Mr. Lincoln more than 624,000 times. That's how many sons and brothers and husbands whose lives were claimed, North and South, during his time in the White House.

And don't for a moment think he did not experience those deaths in a personal way; did not grieve as a mother or father would grieve for a son, or a wife would grieve for a husband. Each soldier's death claimed a piece of his heart as sure as Ann Rutledge claimed her fair share.

Here is an example. Amidst all his troubles Lincoln took time to compose a letter to a young girl on the death of her father in the war. The girl suffered depression similar to that of the Lincolns upon the death of Willie the previous February:

LINCOLN

It is with deep grief that I learn of the death of your kind and brave Father; and, especially, that it is affecting your young heart beyond what is common in such cases.

In this sad world of ours, sorrow comes to all; and, to the young, it comes with bitterest agony, because it takes them unawares. The older have learned to ever expect it. I am anxious to afford some alleviation of your present distress. Perfect relief is not possible, except with time. You can not now realize that you will ever feel better. Is not this so? And yet it is a mistake. You are sure to be happy again. To know this, which is certainly true, will make you some less miserable now. I have had experience enough to know what

I say; and you need only to believe it, to feel better at once. The memory of your dear Father instead of an agony will yet be a sad sweet feeling in your heart, of a purer, and holier sort than you have known before.

READER

The Generals often scolded Lincoln for his leniency; it was "destroying the discipline of the Army" and he must keep his hands off. But in times of war, Presidents have enormous powers; and he could override any judgment or verdict handed down by the military courts.

He hated the brutal methods of the brigadier generals, and the despotism of the regular army. On the other hand, he loved the volunteers on whom he had to depend for winning the war – men who, like himself, had come from the forest and farm. When one of them was to be shot for cowardice, he said: "Did not God give us two good legs to run with? And I'm to abide by executing a man who runs impulsively? I have never been sure but that I might drop my gun and run myself if I were in battle."

A mere list of his pardons would fill many pages. On one day alone he pardoned 63 soldiers. Of course each one required a good deal of paperwork; reading over the particulars, weighing each case against the others. On some days he would work on these pardons well into the night.

One such occasion was for a solider sentenced to death for sleeping at his post. He was but 19 and the only son of a widowed mother. He was well thought of by his comrades who telegraphed his mother about his fate. She employed a friend to travel to Washington. This friend, who was no more than a messenger, really, arrived in that city at Midnight and the soldier was to be executed in the afternoon of the next day. With letter in hand, he was allowed past the military guard at the White House and made it to the doorkeeper, who took him straight to Mr. Lincoln's sleeping room.

The President sent an aide to the war department close by to send a telegram to stay the execution; but growing uneasy by the length of time it took, he dressed, went to the department, and remained there until receipt of his telegram was confirmed. Then he turned to the messenger and said, "Now you just telegraph that mother that her boy is safe, and I will go home and go to bed. I guess we shall all sleep better for this night's work."

We hear sounds of DRUM in background, sounding a funeral cadence. DRUMS recede.

READER

In the swamp, in secluded recesses,
A shy and hidden bird is warbling a song.
Solitary, the thrush, the hermit, withdrawn to himself,
Avoiding the settlements, sings by himself a song.
Song of the bleeding throat! Death's outlet song of life —
(For well, dear brother, I know If thou wast not gifted to sing,
thou would'st surely die.)

Over the breast of the spring, the land, amid cities,
Amid lanes, and through old woods, (where lately the violets
peep'd from the ground, spotting the gray debris;)
Amid the grass in the fields each side of the lanes —
Passing the endless grass; passing the yellow-spear'd wheat,
Every grain from its shroud in the dark-brown fields uprising;
Passing the apple-tree blows of white and pink in the
orchards; carrying a corpse to where it shall rest in the grave,
night and day journeys a coffin.

Coffin that passes through lanes and streets,
Through day and night, with the great cloud darkening the land,
With the pomp of the inloop'd flags, with the cities draped in black,
With the show of the States themselves, as of crape-veil'd women, standing,

With processions long and winding, and the flambeaus of the night,
With the countless torches lit — with the silent sea of faces, and the unbared heads,
With the waiting depot, the arriving coffin, and the sombre faces,
With dirges through the night, with the thousand voices rising strong and solemn;
With All the mournful voices of the dirges, pour'd around the coffin,
The dim-lit churches and the shuddering organs —
Where amid these you journey, with the tolling, tolling bells' perpetual clang;
Here! coffin that slowly passes, I give you my sprig of lilac.

(Nor for you, for one, alone; blossoms and branches green to coffins all I bring:
For fresh as the morning — thus would I carol a song for you,
O sane and sacred death. All over bouquets of roses,
O death! I cover you over with roses and early lilies;
But mostly and now the lilac that blooms the first,
Copious, I break, I break the sprigs from the bushes;
With loaded arms I come, pouring for you,
For you, and the coffins all of you, O death.)

DRUM ROLL

READER

I knew Lincoln well. Came to Springfield in 1836 or 37, we had some business dealings for a couple of years. Ran for political office several times — was beaten more often than not, which was fine with me. Lincoln was a gloomy man—a sad man. His wife, Mary Todd, made him president: she had the fire—will and ambition—Lincoln's talent and his wife's ambition did the deed—Lincoln courted several ladies. They all refused him. Lincoln is—was, a kind of vegetable—that needed driving. [laughs] Well, he got that. He was a very domestic man—a torpid man, gloomy. Lincoln's peculiar constitution—his dormancy—his vegetable constitution, his want of passion—emotion—imagination…how he was elected president, I'll never know. By all rights, he should have died—been killed in the first three months. But I'll give him this, he was tough and enduring.

Lincoln did forget his friends—there was no part of his nature which drew him to do acts of gratitude to his friends. Lincoln was an educated man, though he dug it out of himself—Shakespeare; he could well repeat much of Shakespeare.

The marriage of Lincoln to Miss Todd was a policy match all around—Lincoln was not a social man—was sad, gloomy, he couldn't care for any man's interest—tended to no public interest—those things that interest the unpolitical public—cared nothing for colleges, railroads, churches, hospitals, and such like things and institutions, attended no such meetings, had no organizing abilities—felt no special interest in any man or thing—save and except politics—loved principles and such—like large political and national ones, especially when it leads to his own ends—ambitions—success. So, that's your honest Abe for you.

COMMENTATOR

Well I guess my friend's words only prove what Mr. Lincoln would often say - that is; you can't please all of the people all of the time.

Much has been written about Mr. Lincoln's physical appearance. To put it mildly he was not a handsome man. Of this fact he was well aware.

He once said: "If any personal description of me is thought desirable, it may be said I am, in height, six feet four inches nearly, lean in flesh, weighing on an average 180 pounds, dark complexion with course, black hair and grey eyes — no other marks or brand recollected."

He once commented that, because of his looks, he felt uncomfortable in the company of attractive women: "I feel like the ugly man riding through a wood who meets a woman, also on horseback, who stops and says to me; 'Well, for land sake you are the homeliest man I ever saw.' I would say 'Yes, madam, but I can't help it,' 'No, I suppose not,' she says, 'but you might try staying at home.'"

READER

A yarn is told of him that on one occasion he was splitting rails (by his own account, from the time he was nine until in his twenties, he was never without an axe in his hand.) On this occasion, with only shirt-collar open and britches on, a man happened to be passing with a gun and called to Lincoln to look up — which he did, and the man raised his gun in an attitude to shoot. Says Lincoln, "What do you mean by pointing that gun at me!" The man replied that he had promised to shoot the first man he met who was uglier than himself. Lincoln asked the man to step forward so he could see his face better, and after taking a good long look remarked, "If I am uglier than you, then shoot away."

READER

He didn't go to see the girls much. He didn't appear bashful, but it seemed as if he cared but little for them. Wasn't apt to take liberties with them, but would sometimes. Mr. Lincoln used to tell the following anecdote of himself. Once, when he was out on the road surveying, he was given board in the same room with two girls—the head of his bed being next to the foot of the girls' bed.

In the night, he commenced tickling the feet of one of the girls with his fingers. As she seemed to enjoy it as much as he did, he then tickled a little higher up; and as he would tickle higher, the girl would shove down lower, and the higher he tickled, the lower she moved. Mr. Lincoln would tell the story with evident enjoyment, but he never told how the thing ended.

READER

One morning Lincoln came to my office and joined me in a game of chess. We were both enthusiastic chess players, and when the opportunity offered, we would indulge in a game. On this occasion, we were soon deeply involved and did not realize how near it was to the noon hour, until one of Lincoln's young sons came running with the message from his mother announcing dinner at the Lincoln home, a few steps away. Lincoln promised to come at once and the boy left. But the game was not entirely over. Yet so near the end, we were confident we could finish it in a few moments. So we lingered awhile. Meanwhile, almost half an hour passed. Presently the boy returned with a second and more urgent call for dinner; but so deeply engrossed in the game we were, that we failed to notice his arrival.

This was more than the little fellow could stand; so that, angered at our inattention, he moved nearer, lifted his foot, and deliberately kicked the board, chessmen and all, went flying into the air.

It was one of the most abrupt, if not brazen things I ever saw. But the surprising thing was its effect on Lincoln. Instead of the animated scene between an irate father and an imprudent youth, which I expected, Mr. Lincoln, without a word of reproof, calmly arose, took the boy by the hand, and started for dinner.

Reaching the door, he turned, smiled good naturedly, and exclaimed, "Well, I reckon we'll have to finish this game some other time," and passed out the door.

Refrain of FUNERAL DRUM CADENCE is heard. DRUM ENDS.

READER

Sing on, there in the swamp! O singer bashful and tender! I hear your notes — I hear your call; I hear — I come presently — I understand you; But a moment I linger — for the lustrous star has detain'd me; The star, my departing comrade, holds and detains me.
O how shall I warble myself for the dead one there I loved? And how shall I deck my song for the large sweet soul that has gone? And what shall my perfume be, for the grave of him I love? Sea-winds, blown from east and west, Blown from the eastern sea, and blown from the western sea, till there on the prairies meeting: These, and with these, and the breath of my chant, I perfume the grave of him I love.

Sing on! sing on, you gray-brown bird! Sing from the swamps, the recesses — pour your chant from the bushes; limitless out of the dusk, out of the cedars and pines. Sing on, dearest brother —

warble your reedy song;lLoud human song, with voice of uttermost woe. O liquid, and free, and tender! O wild and loose to my soul! O wondrous singer! You only I hear......yet the star holds me, (but will soon depart ;)
Yet the lilac, with mastering odor, holds me.

COMMENTATOR

By the time of Mr. Lincoln's inauguration in March of 1861, the country was already in a fractured condition. When he, a known opponent of slavery, was elected president, the South Carolina legislature perceived a threat. Calling a state convention, the delegates voted to remove the state of South Carolina from the union known as the United States of America.

The secession of South Carolina was followed by the secession of six more states --Mississippi, Florida, Alabama, Georgia, Louisiana, and Texas. Virginia, Arkansas, Tennessee, and North Carolina soon followed suit. These eleven states eventually formed the Confederate States of America.

Mr. Lincoln had hoped to resolve this national crisis without warfare. All that changed on April 12th with the attack on Federal troops occupying Ft. Sumter. The President's worst fears were realized. America was at war with itself. But even in this grim reality the hopes of many, including the President, remained heightened with the belief that the war would be brief and last no longer than six months.

From the beginning, fate would work against a quick resolution. The legendary Field General, Robert E. Lee, would take command of the Confederate Armies, while on the Union side no such effective leader emerged. And so the war dragged on.

LINCOLN

The will of God prevails. In great contests each party claims to act in accordance with the will of God. Both may be, and one must be, wrong. God cannot be for and against the same thing at the same time. In the present civil war, it is quite possible that God's purpose is something different from the purpose of either party — and yet the human instrumentalities, working just as they do, are of the best adaptation to effect his purpose.

I am almost ready to say this is probably true — that God wills this contest, and wills that it shall not end yet. By his mere quiet power, on the minds of the now contestants, He could have either saved or destroyed the Union without a human contest. Yet the contest began. And having begun, He could give the final victory to either side any day. Yet the contest proceeds.

What is to be will be, and no prayers of ours can arrest this decree.

COMMENTATOR

At precisely the time when the war demanded all of Mr. Lincoln's attention and energies, a terrible tragedy befell him and his family.

In the winter of 1862, his eleven-year-old son Willie died of typhoid fever. The president was at his bedside and broke down and cried. After spending some time alone with Willie, the president went back to his desk and continued working.

READER

I was the first one to see Mr. Lincoln after he left Willie's room. He stopped as he drew near to me and said simply "He's gone, he's actually gone." Then he passed on to his office and continued on with his presidential duties.

He found it difficult to accept his son's loss. Eventually, his grief transformed into a personal resolution to preserve the Union and halt the loss of life soldiers and their families were experiencing. I remember something he said shortly after his son's death -

"I believe it is the invincible right of man to be happy or miserable of his own decision, and I, for one, make the choice for the former."

He also said something curious to me some time later, which stayed with me always. I was alone with him in his office when he disassociated from our conversation and remarked to me about a change that had come over him.

He said, while he could not remember any precise time when he passed through any special change of purpose, or of heart, yet it was after he came here, and I am very positive that in his own mind he identified it with about the time of Willie's death.

He called this change "a process of crystallization" that had gone on in his mind. As I understood it, the change he referred to was of a spiritual nature.

He said, too, that after he moved to the White House he kept up the habit of daily prayer. Sometimes he said it was only ten words, but those ten words he faithfully practiced.

COMMENTATOR

I shared an office with Mr. Lincoln in Springfield, Ill. for some years. At the time, I was a voracious reader. If I happened to come across a noteworthy book that I believed Mr. Lincoln would benefit from reading I would place it on a commonly shared table in the center of the room. Once I placed a copy of the newly published *Leaves of Grass* on the table.

As Mr. Lincoln was leaving, he noticed the book, stopped and picked it up. He was particularly moved by an introduction letter to the author written by R.W. Emerson.

He leafed through the book, stopped at Emerson's letter and quoted him out loud – "I greet you at the beginning of a great career" - "I find it the most extraordinary piece of wit and wisdom that America has yet contributed."

"Well, Bill, said Mr. Lincoln, if Walt Whitman's good enough for Emerson, he's good enough for me." He then tucked the book under his arm and departed.

Later, when visiting Mr. Lincoln at his home, on more than one occasion, I happened to see the opened book of *Leaves of Grass* on his night stand.

WHITMAN & FRIEND

FRIEND

Here we are Walt, at the foot of the Great Mansion itself. Sometimes I think you rent a room close to here just so you can get your daily look at the President. Sometimes I think you came to Washington just to be near him. There he is, greeting the throngs as usual, like he's bosom buddies with each one of them personally. Let's go over and shake his hand; you could introduce yourself as Walt Whitman, the Great Dramatic Poet.

WHITMAN

Very funny but no, I'm too shabbily dressed today to greet him.

FRIEND

Walt, you're always shabbily dressed, that's no excuse.

WHITMAN

There will be other times to meet him, and much better occasions than having to wait in line with so many other people for the privilege of five seconds of the President's attention.

Lincoln is particularly my man — particularly belongs to me; yes, and by the same token, I am Lincoln's man: I guess I particularly belong to him; we are afloat on the same stream — we are rooted in the same ground. There'll be other times for our meeting.

LINCOLN & FRIEND

FRIEND

Yes Mr. President?

LINCOLN

Do you see those two men across the street, the ones now

walking away? That one, with the white hair and open collar, I've seen him before; do you know his name?

FRIEND

If I'm not mistaken, Mr. President, that's the poet, Walt Whitman.

LINCOLN

Walt Whitman. Well, there goes a real man.

COMMENTATOR

Nothing impressed me more with Mr. Lincoln than his remarkable talent for rendering things in their most simplistic terms. Simplicity, for him, was a way of life. He himself considered it one of man's great virtues.

On the issue of Slavery, certainly one of the most debated, discussed, evaluated issues of any period in this country's history, he possessed the ability to distill it to a couple of short sentences. (Reads from letter)

> "I never knew a man who wished to be himself, a slave.
> Consider if you know any good thing that no man
> desires for himself."

This same simplicity is readily apparent in what is perhaps one of the most remarkable speeches ever uttered by a man from any nation of the world, in any era. It has come to be known in these times as *The Gettysburg Address,* after the battle of Gettysburg; considered by many to be the defining moment in the war - the battle that turned the tide over to the union's favor.

The fighting began on July 1st 1863 and quite fittingly ended three days later on July 4th, with the Confederate army's retreat. In those three days, the combined loss of life of the Union and Confederate armies amounted to no less than 50,000 men. Although both sides suffered similar numbers of loses, it was for the Confederate side a defeat from which they were never to recover.

President Lincoln arrived at Gettysburg, Pennsylvania in November of 1863, four months after the bloody battle. The townsfolk of Gettysburg built a cemetery for the dead soldiers. There was to be a dedication. A local attorney had invited Lincoln to offer a "few appropriate remarks" after the main speech by Edward Everett, a renowned orator. Everett spoke to the crowd of 15,000 assembled in the Soldiers' National Cemetery for two hours before Lincoln's remarks, which lasted only two or three minutes.

LINCOLN

Four score and seven years ago, our fathers brought forth on this continent a new nation: conceived in liberty, and dedicated to the proposition that all men are created equal.

Now we are engaged in a great civil war ... testing whether that nation or any nation so conceived and so dedicated ... can long endure. We are met on a great buttlefield of that war.

We have come to dedicate a portion of that field as a final resting place for those who here gave their lives that that nation might live. It is altogether fitting and proper that we should do this.

But, in a larger sense, we cannot dedicate ... we cannot consecrate ... we cannot hallow this ground. The brave men, living and dead, who struggled here, have consecrated it far above our poor power to add or detract.

The world will little note, nor long remember, what we say here, but it can never forget what they did here. It is for us the living, rather, to be dedicated here to the unfinished work which they who fought here have thus far so nobly advanced.

It is rather for us to be here dedicated to the great task remaining before us ... that from these honored dead we take increased devotion to that cause for which they gave the last full measure of devotion ... that we here highly resolve that these dead shall not have died in vain ...

That this nation, under God, shall have a new birth of freedom ... and that government of the people ... by the people ... for the people ... shall not perish from the earth.

GRANT

My military career was rather ho-hum until Mr. Lincoln asked me to replace General McClellan in 1864. I guess he felt like there was nothing much to lose; McClellan being so indecisive as to be practically a non-combatant. He flatly refused the President's continued urgings to pursue the Confederate Army that was closing in on Washington.

Finally, the President got so fed up with him, he sent a message to this effect – "Gen. McClellan, may I borrow your army; it appears you are not using it at the moment." Of course that remark became well known and often repeated among the troops, who got a good laugh from it; but the gravity of the situation remained.

Something had to be done and I was sent word I would be McClellan's replacement.

I didn't have the best reputation at the time, and the President took a lot of abuse for appointing me Commander of the Union Army. The word was I drank too much. Maybe I did. In those times many a good man felt the need to block out the war; more so, if you were smack dab in the middle of it. My drinking habit was once brought by a cabinet member before the President and he reputedly said –"Find out what Grant's drinking and send some of it to the other generals."

I remember the first time I met the President. I had just received news of my appointment and was called to the White house and ushered straight to the President where a reception was in full swing. As I entered into the brightly lighted East Room it seemed as if the room went silent. The president turned to a guest and excused himself and approached me. He put out that long arm and said "General, I'm glad to see you." From that moment on, he always showed me the greatest respect.

He told me he did not want to know what I proposed to do. But he would submit to me a plan of his own that he wanted me to consider and then do as I thought best.

Here is the first note I received from him:
(Reads from Note)

> "You are vigilant and self-reliant; and, pleased with this, I wish not to obtrude any constraints or restraints upon you. While I am very anxious that any great disaster or capture of our men in great numbers shall be avoided, I know these points are less likely to escape your attention than they would be mine. If there is anything wanting which is within my power to give, do not fail to let me know it. And now, with a brave army and a just cause, may God sustain you."

Looking back, I only regret not being with him on the night he was killed. Perhaps things would have been different. He invited my wife and me to accompany him and Mrs. Lincoln to Ford's Theater. My wife did not get on well with Mrs. Lincoln and so she refused to go. I declined the invitation giving some sort of lame excuse which he gracefully accepted. There are times still I wonder "what if I had been in that room with him; would anything have been different, averted?" We'll never know.

COMMENTATOR

As the war raged on, Mr. Lincoln spent more and more time at the War Department; reading the latest dispatches from the front and conferring with officers.

The day he was nominated for a second term, someone had to go there and inform him of this fact. Looking back on this time, I see now how much he changed. He seemed to have aged 20 years since he took office. Suddenly I remember looking at him and realizing his was the saddest face I ever knew. There were days when I could scarcely look into it without crying.

As the Union losses mounted, General Grant suddenly stood again where all the previous commanders had stood, most recently McClellan. Grant stood there defeated. He could think of nothing to do but just what McClellan did — abandon the immediate enterprise, make a great retreat, and start a new campaign on a different plan.

Four years with all the terrible disasters, and this was all that had come of it! Practically no gain, and a death-roll that staggered the nation. A wail went over the North. After all, was the war hopeless? Was Lee invincible? Was the whole race of man the North had to offer perishing to no result?

GRANT

But in fact, I didn't retreat – I went against my own better judgment and the judgment of most of my peers and advanced; I could sense in every fiber of my being that the end was near and victory would be ours.

COMMENTATOR

General Grant's intuitions were correct. The Union would gain control of the Mississippi River at the battle of Vicksburg, essentially splitting the South in half. In 1865, Lee tried to outrun Grant toward Richmond; but after a long siege, the Union troops breached the defenses and forced Lee to retreat. The Confederates moved along the Appomattox River, with the Union in pursuit. Lee's army did not have much food left, and the troops started to desert in large numbers. When Lee arrived at Appomattox, his path was blocked, so he asked for a meeting with Grant.

They met at 2:00 p.m. on April 9 1865. They spoke briefly and cordially of their previous service in the Mexican War. Oddly enough, the surrender took place in the home of a local farmer.

He had lived along the banks of Bull Run, the site of the first major battle in 1861. Seeing his town devastated by the battle he moved to avoid any future fighting. He moved to Appomattox, only to see the war end in his living room.

Grant offered generous terms: Officers could keep their side arms, and all soldiers would be released immediately. Officers and enlisted men who owned horses could keep them to plant crops and see their families through the winter.

These terms, Lee said, would have "the best possible effect upon the men" and "will do much toward conciliating our people." The papers were signed and Lee departed after the two-hour meeting. As he passed his troops with tears streaming down his face, he said: "Men, we have fought through the war together. I have done the best that I could for you."

The United State's Civil War had come to an end.

Word of Lee's surrender spread quickly. On the following day, the mood around the Capital was buoyant and cheerful. A large crowd, including a brass band, gathered near the President's balcony and clamored for his appearance. Mr. Lincoln made his way through the throng of well wishers and surprised everyone by asking the band to play *Dixie*, the unofficial Anthem of the Confederacy.

He did this not as a way of chiding the vanquished South, nor to appease them. But in his simple straight forward manner, he confessed that *Dixie* was always one of his favorite tunes and although the South had claimed it as its own, he saw it as purely American. Perhaps this was his very first act to re-unify the country.

SINGER

Oh, I wish I was in the land of cotton,
Old times there are not forgotten,
Look away, look away, look away Dixie Land.

I wish I was in Dixie, Hooray! Hooray!
In Dixie Land I'll take my stand
to live and die in Dixie.
Away, away, away down south in Dixie.
Away, away, away down south in Dixie.

In Dixie Land, where I was born in,
early on one frosty mornin',
Look away, look away, look away Dixie Land.

I wish I was in Dixie, Hooray! Hooray!
In Dixie Land I'll take my stand
to live and die in Dixie.
Away, away, away down south in Dixie.
Away, away, away down south in Dixie.

COMMENTATOR

There were several strange and ominous events that occurred just prior to Mr. Lincoln's death on April 15th 1865. A few related to dreams he had had. The night before his assassination he had a dream which he relayed to his cabinet the next morning, just hours before the assassination. In this dream he saw himself "in a singular and indescribable vessel, but always the same...moving with great rapidity toward a dark and indefinite shore." Mr. Lincoln had this same dream numerous times but always before a great Union victory on the battlefield. "Gentleman," he said, "because of this dream, I feel we are on the cusp of a very important event."

But the most startling incident occurred a few nights prior. He related this dream in the presence of myself and his wife.

LINCOLN

"About ten days ago, I retired very late. I had been up waiting for important dispatches from the front. I could not have been long in bed, when I fell into a slumber, for I was weary. I soon began to dream. There seemed to be a death-like stillness about me. Then I heard subdued sobs, as if a number of people were weeping. I thought I left my bed and wandered downstairs. There the silence was broken by the same pitiful sobbing, but the mourners were invisible. I went from room to room; no living person was in sight, but the same mournful sounds of distress met me as I passed along. It was light in all the rooms; every object was familiar to me; but where were all the people who were grieving as if their hearts would break? I was puzzled and alarmed.

What could be the meaning of all this? Determined to find the cause of a state of things so mysterious and so shocking, I kept on until I arrived at the East Room, which I entered. There I met with a sickening surprise. Before me was a catafalque, on which rested a corpse wrapped in funeral vestments.

Around it were stationed soldiers who were acting as guards; and there was a throng of people, some gazing mournfully upon the corpse, whose face was covered, others weeping pitifully. 'Who is dead in the White House?' I demanded of one of the soldiers. 'The President,' was his answer; 'He was killed by an assassin!' Then came a loud burst of grief from the crowd, which awoke me from my dream. I slept no more that night; and although it was only a dream, I have been strangely annoyed by it ever since."

COMMENTATOR

He also related to me that after waking from this dream, he went to his bible, picked it up, and started leafing through the pages.

LINCOLN

"The first time I opened the Bible, strange as it may appear, it was at the twenty-eighth chapter of Genesis which relates the wonderful dream Jacob had. I turned to other passages and seemed to encounter a dream or a vision wherever I looked. I kept on turning the leaves of the Old Book, and everywhere my eye fell upon passages recording matters strangely in keeping with my own thoughts--supernatural visitations, dreams, visions, etc."

COMMENTATOR

There lived in Washington D C, an actor from a prominent British family of actors. Very charismatic and handsome, he reminded some of Byron in beauty and temperament, except perhaps with more than a dash of insanity. His name was John Wilkes Booth and being a violent secessionist, he had long meditated killing the President. In his morbid imagination, he had made of Lincoln another Caesar. The occasion called for a Brutus.

That occasion turned out to be Good Friday, April 14th 1865, at Ford's theater, during a performance of *Our American Cousin*, a farcical, light hearted play that had received good reviews in the local papers.

READER

After an afternoon carriage ride and dinner with the President, Mrs. Lincoln complained of a headache and considered not going to the theater after all. Mr. Lincoln commented that he was feeling a bit tired himself, but he needed a laugh and was intent on going with or without her.

She relented. He made a quick trip to the War Department with his body guard, William Crook, but there was no news to speak of, all was quiet on the front. Crook, one of the president's personal guards almost begged Mr. Lincoln not to go to the theater. He then asked if he could go along as an extra guard. Mr. Lincoln rejected both suggestions, shrugging off Crook's fears he would be in danger.

COMMENTATOR

Besides General Grant and his wife, eleven others turned down Mr. Lincoln's invitation to join him in the Presidential Box that night. With the President and his wife, were one other couple; a young Military Officer and his fiancée, the daughter of a Senator.

John Wilkes Booth, who knew the theater well, slipped in a back door and made his way unnoticed to the door of the Presidential suite. It was closed but not locked. There was an empty chair positioned right outside the door, which should have been occupied by the guard assigned to protect the President that night. Booth slowly turned the knob, entered, and encountered Mr. Lincoln first, seated directly in front of him.

He fired one round at point blank range into the President, stabbed the young officer in the arm and leaped off the railing onto the stage below. Some say as he regained his balance, for he broke his leg while landing awkwardly, he cried out "Sic semper tyrannis!"- Thus it is with tyrants, and fled back stage to the outside through the same door he entered.

JOHN PARKER

My name is John Parker. I was on duty as the President's guard the night he was murdered. I was supposed to be guarding the door to the state box that night but... well, what happened was... I couldn't see a damned thing from that hallway, so I went out in the auditorium to get a better view; with all the laughing going on, I didn't want to miss such a good show. At the intermission, I saw a few friends who invited me to the saloon next door.

Strangest thing happened, while I was in the saloon, I looked down to the end of the bar and saw John Wilkes Booth sitting alone. Everyone who went to the theater knew him well; he was usually holding court with a group of hanger's on, but that night he was sittin' there kind of quiet like. He left around ten. Looking back, I guess he needed the alcohol to give him the courage to do what he intended.

At the saloon, I met a lady friend; and well, I never made it back to the theater that night—didn't hear of Mr. Lincoln's death until the next day. A few days later, I was guarding at the White House and Mrs. Lincoln really lit into me.

MRS. LINCOLN

So you are on guard tonight - on guard in the White House after helping to murder the President!

JOHN PARKER

I don't blame her for being upset, I admit I hadn't done my duty that night; but she had no right to accuse me of murdering the President. Like I told her, I was attracted by the play, and did not see the assassin enter the box. But I did not help to murder the President. I could never stoop to murder--much less to the murder of so good and great a man as the President. He always treated me kindly; I never would have intentionally done anything to harm him.

COMMENTATOR

John Parker was a Washington D. C. police officer on special assignment to guard the President. He was fired from the police force a few months later, when he was found sleeping on duty.

The bullet of the assassin had entered the brain, causing the President to instantly lapse into a coma. He was removed to a house across the street from the theater where he was laid on a bed. Swift panic took possession of the city. A crowd of people rushed instinctively to the White House, and bursting through the doors, shouted the dreadful news to Robert Lincoln, the President's oldest son, himself just returned from the war.

He was taken by carriage to the location where his father lay dying, and where he met his grief stricken mother who was overcome with emotion.

Around dawn, the President's pulse began to fail. A little later a look of unspeakable peace came over his worn features.

READER

The President is Dead – Abraham Lincoln died this morning at twenty-two minutes past seven o'clock.

SARAH BUSH LINCOLN

My name is Sarah Bush Lincoln. I was Mr. Lincoln's stepmother. I was a widow, already with three of my own children. Abe was then nine years old and his sister eleven. I dressed them both up, made them look more human. The country was wild and desolate. Abe was a good boy; was thirsty for knowledge, wished to know everything. He was the best boy I ever saw.

Abe read the Bible some. When newspapers were had in Indiana, Abe was a constant reader of them. Abe had no particular religion—didn't think of that question at the time. If he did, he never talked about it. Abe, when old folks were at our house, was a silent and attentive observer, never speaking or asking questions till they were gone, and then he must understand everything—even to the smallest detail, minutely and exactly. He would then repeat it over to himself again and again, and when it was fixed in his mind, he never lost that fact or his understanding of it. He would hear sermons preached, come home, take the children out, get on a stump or log, and almost repeat it word for word. His father made him quit sometimes, as he neglected his own work to speak and made the other children neglect their work as well. But overall, Abe's father was proud of him. He encouraged Abraham to learn in any way he could. Abe was a poor boy, and I can say what scarcely one mother can say in a thousand, and it is this—Abe never gave me a cross word or look and never refused in fact, or even in appearance, to do anything I requested him.

He was kind to everybody and everything, and always accommodates others if he could—would do so willingly, if he could. Abe was always fond of fun—sport and jokes—he was sometimes very witty indeed. He never drank whiskey, was temperate in all things—too much so, I thought sometimes. He never told me a lie in his life—never evaded, never equivocated, never dodged—nor turned a corner to avoid any chastisement or other responsibility.

Abe loved me truly, I think. I had a son, John, who was raised with Abe. Both were good boys, but I must say—both now being dead, that Abe was the best boy I ever saw or expect to see.

I did not want Abe to run for president—did not want him elected—was afraid somehow or other—felt it in my heart that something would happen to him, and when he came down to see me after he was elected President, I still felt that something would befall Abe and that I should see him no more. Abe and his father are in heaven, I have not doubt, and I want to go there—go where they are. God bless Abraham.

COMMENTATOR

On April 14th, 1879, Walt Whitman delivered in New York City a lecture commemorating the 15th anniversary of Mr. Lincoln's death.

WHITMAN

I shall not easily forget the first time I ever saw Abraham Lincoln. It must have been about the 18th or 19th of February, 1861. It was rather a pleasant afternoon, in New York City, as he arrived there from the West to remain a few hours, and then pass on to Washington to prepare for his inauguration.

I saw him in Broadway. He came down, I think from Canal street, to stop at the Astor House. The sidewalks were crowded with solid masses of people, many thousands. The omnibuses and other vehicles had all been turn'd off, leaving an unusual hush in that busy part of the city. Presently, two or three carriages made their way with some difficulty through the crowd and drew up at the Astor House entrance.

A tall figure step'd out of one the these carriages, paus'd leisurely on the sidewalk, look'd up at the granite walls and looming architecture of the grand old hotel—then, after a relieving stretch of arms and legs, turn'd round for over a minute to slowly and good-humoredly scan the appearance of the vast and silent crowds. There were no speeches—no compliments—no welcome—as far as I could hear, not a word said. Still much anxiety was conceal'd in that quiet.

Cautious persons had fear'd some mark'd insult or indignity to the President-elect—for he possess'd no personal popularity at all in New York City, and very little political. But it was evidently tacitly agreed that if the few political supporters of Mr. Lincoln present would entirely abstain from any demonstration on their side, the immense majority, who were any thing but supporters, would abstain on their side also. The result was a sulky, unbroken silence, such as certainly never before characterized so great a New York crowd.

From the top of an omnibus, I had, I say, a capital view of it all, and especially of Mr. Lincoln, his look and gait—his perfect composure and coolness—his unusual and uncouth height, his dress of complete black, stovepipe hat push'd back on the head, dark-brown complexion, seam'd and wrinkled yet canny-looking face, black, bushy head of hair, disproportionately long neck, and his hands held behind as he stood observing the people. He look'd with curiosity upon that immense sea of faces, and the sea of faces return'd the look with similar curiosity.

  In both there was a dash of comedy, almost farce, such as Shakespeare puts in his blackest tragedies. The crowd that hemm'd around consisted I should think of thirty to forty thousand men, not a single one his personal friend—while I have no doubt, (so frenzied were the ferments of the time,) many an assassin's knife and pistol lurk'd in hip or breast-pocket there, ready, soon as break and riot came.

But no break or riot came. The tall figure gave another relieving stretch or two of arms and legs; then with moderate pace, and accompanied by a few unknown looking persons, ascended the portico-steps of the Astor House and disappear'd through its broad entrance.

READER

Come, lovely and soothing Death, Undulate round the world, serenely arriving, arriving, In the day, in the night, to all, to each, Sooner or later, delicate Death.
Prais'd be the fathomless universe, for life and joy, and for

objects
and knowledge curious; and for love, sweet love — but praise!
Praise! Praise!
For the sure-enwinding arms of cool-enfolding Death.
Dark Mother, always gliding near, with soft feet,
Have none chanted for thee a chant of fullest welcome?
Then I chant it for thee — I glorify thee above all; I bring thee a song

That when thou must indeed come, come
unfalteringly. Approach strong deliveress!
When it is so — when thou hast taken them, I joyously sing the dead, lost in the loving, floating ocean of thee, laved in the flood of thy bliss, O Death.

From me to thee glad serenades, dances for thee I propose,
saluting thee — adornments and feastings for thee; And the sights
of the open landscape, and the high-spread sky,
are fitting, and life and the fields, and the huge and thoughtful night.

The night, in silence, under many a star; The ocean shore, and
the husky whispering wave, whose voice I know; And the soul
turning to thee, O vast and well-veil'd Death, And the body
gratefully nestling close to thee. Over the tree-tops I float thee a song!
Over the rising and sinking waves — over the myriad fields, and the prairies wide;
Over the dense-pack'd cities all, and the teeming wharves and ways,
I float this carol with joy, with joy to thee, O Death!

To the tally of my soul, loud and strong kept up the gray-brown bird, with pure, deliberate notes, spreading, filling the night. Loud in the pines and cedars dim, clear in the freshness moist, and the swamp-perfume; And I with my comrades there in the night.
While my sight that was bound in my eyes unclosed, as to long

panoramas of visions.

I saw askant the armies; and I saw, as in noiseless dreams,
Hundreds of battle-flags; borne through the smoke of the battles,
And pierc'd with missiles, I saw them, and carried hither and
yon through the smoke, and torn and bloody; And at last but a
few shreds left on the staffs, (and all in silence,) and the staffs all
splinter'd and broken.
I saw battle-corpses, myriads of them, and the white skeletons
of young men—I saw them; I saw the debris and debris of all the
dead soldiers of the war; but I saw they were not as was thought;
they themselves were fully at rest—they suffer'd not;
The living remain'd and suffer'd—the mother suffer'd,
And the wife and the child, and the musing comrade suffer'd,
And the armies that remain'd suffer'd.

Passing the visions, passing the night; passing, unloosing the
hold
of my comrades' hands; passing the song of the hermit bird,
and the tallying song of my soul,
(Victorious song, death's outlet song, yet varying, ever-altering
song,
As low and wailing, yet clear the notes, rising and falling,
flooding the night,

Sadly sinking and fainting, as warning and warning,
and yet again bursting with joy, covering the earth,
and filling the spread of the heaven,
As that powerful psalm in the night I heard from recesses,)
Passing, I leave thee, lilac with heart-shaped leaves;
I leave thee there in the door-yard, blooming, returning with
spring,
I cease from my song for thee; from my gaze on thee in the west,
fronting
the west, Communing with thee, O comrade lustrous,
with silver face in the night.

Yet each I keep, and all, retrievements out of the night;
The song, the wondrous chant of the gray-brown
bird, And the tallying chant,
The echo arous'd in my soul, with the lustrous and
drooping star,
With the countenance full of woe, with the lilac tall, and its
blossoms of mastering odor;

With the holders holding my hand, nearing the call of the
bird, comrades mine,
And I in the midst, and their memory ever I keep—for the dead
I loved so well;
For the sweetest, wisest soul of all my days and lands...
and this for his dear sake;
Lilac and star and bird, twined with the chant of my soul,
There in the fragrant pines, and the cedars dusk and dim.

DRUM – FUNERAL CADENCE BEGINS, SLOWS AND
FADES OUT.

THE END

download Volume 2: Whirling Dervishes
and the Kaaba Inside

Abraham Lincoln

Live Performance of *A. Lincoln:
This Dust Was Once The Man,* July 4, 2011
Leonard Hill (above) as Lincoln

Mari Reeves recites
When Lilacs Last in the Dooryard Bloom'd

Christopher King as Narrator

Robert George as William Herndon

*http://bluelogic.us/pages/34-1031.php
for Volume 2: Whirling Dervishes
and the Kaaba Inside*

http://livingpresence.com

www.ingramcontent.com/pod-product-compliance
Lightning Source LLC
Chambersburg PA
CBHW072022290426
44109CB00018B/2314